TRAVEL BY SEA

ROBERT J. HOARE

A. & C. BLACK LTD
LONDON

BLACK'S JUNIOR REFERENCE BOOKS

General Editor: R. J. Unstead

FIRST EDITION 1961
SECOND EDITION 1967
(revised by the Publishers)
REPRINTED 1970

© 1967 A. & C. BLACK LTD

ISBN 0 7136 0119 1

ACKNOWLEDGMENTS

Most of the drawings in this book are by Winston Megoran. The other drawings are by J. C. B. Knight and T. L. Poulton.

Grateful acknowledgment is made to the following for their permission to reproduce photographs and other illustrations: Aerofilms Ltd., pages 76(a) and (b); British Hovercraft Corporation Ltd., page 78; The British Museum, pages 35(a), 47; the Cunard Steamship Company, pages 67(a), 78(a); the London Museum, page 5(b); the Mansell Collection, page 16(a); the National Maritime Museum, pages 29(a), 42, 44, 51, 52, 56, 63(a), 65(a) and (b), 70(a); the Nautical Photo Agency, page 73(a); the Radio Times Hulton Picture Library, pages 6(c), 17(c), 21(c), 38(a), 39(a), 61(a), 69(a), 71(b); J. Arthur Rank (Productions) Ltd., page 27(b); the Royal Photographic Society, page 70(b); the Science Museum, pages 14(a), 23(a), 28(a), 30(a), 31(b); the United States Information Service, page 74(b).

The photographs on pages 6(b), 17(a), 20(a), 65(b), and 68(b) are from the Science Museum, Crown Copyright reserved. The photograph on page 32 is from the Science Museum, from the original in the Pepysian Library. The painting reproduced on the cover is from the National Maritime Museum, Greenwich.

PUBLISHED BY A. & C. BLACK LTD., 4 SOHO SQUARE, LONDON W1V 6AD
PRINTED BY MORRISON AND GIBB LTD., LONDON AND EDINBURGH

CONTENTS

PART ONE : SHIPS OF EARLY TIMES

PART TWO : THE AGE OF DISCOVERY

PART THREE : THE GREAT DAYS OF SAIL

PART FOUR : THE AGE OF STEAM

PART ONE : SHIPS OF EARLY TIMES

1. THE FIRST SHIPS

No one knows who were the first people to travel by sea. Indeed no one knows who was the first man to travel on water. It must have been some half-naked savage who sat astride a log and crossed a river on it.

Later on, someone had the idea of scooping out the middle of a log with a stone axe. The result was the dug-out canoe. This was the first ship, for the word " ship " comes from a Latin word meaning " to scoop ".

Dug-outs were used in Britain before the Stone Age. There is in London Museum a dug-out that was found in the mud of the River Thames. It was made from the trunk of an elm

tree. When it was found, it had been buried in the ground for so long that it was turned into stone.

Dug-out canoes are still used today by natives in parts of Africa and in the islands of the Pacific Ocean.

A dug-out canoe found in the River Thames

Early Britons using coracles

At least 700 years before the birth of Christ, there appeared on the River Tigris in Babylonia a small circular boat called a *guffa*. The guffa consisted of a wicker framework covered with skins.

Today, guffas are still in use on the Tigris at Baghdad. But now they are woven from wickerwork interlaced with fibre and made waterproof with a coating of bitumen, which is found locally.

When he came to Britain in 55 B.C. Julius Caesar found the Britons using a similar boat called the *coracle*. Coracles are still used in certain districts in Britain; for example, by salmon fishers on the River Severn and the Wye. Nowadays the frames are covered with tarred canvas instead of skins.

A model of a guffa used on the River Tigris today

A Welsh fisherman carries his coracle down to the river

2. EGYPTIAN SHIPS

The earliest sea-going ships we know of were built in Egypt. Several thousand years before the birth of Christ, the people of Egypt were using the River Nile as a highway. The easiest way to carry things was by water, for the wheel had not yet been invented.

Few trees grow in that hot, dry country. So the Egyptians made bundles of a reed called papyrus and used them to build rafts.

After a time, a platform of reeds was built up at each end of these rafts. Then sides were added so that they became flat-bottomed boats.

The Egyptians next began to build such boats with whatever wood they could obtain. It came mostly from acacia trees in the form of short planks.

This meant that the Egyptian boat-builders were unable to give their boats a keel made from a single piece of timber stretching from bow to stern. The keel is the backbone of a ship. The Egyptian ships had no backbone. They were built in the shape of the reed boats, rising high out of the water in a curve at each end. To support these ends, a rope was fastened between them above the deck of the ship and a piece of wood was fitted in the rope

An Egyptian reed-boat

so that it could be twisted and made tighter.

Because they were raised at both bow and stern and because they rode high in the water, these ships were able to go close to the shore. This made it easier to unload their cargoes.

Building an Egyptian ship

An Egyptian sailing ship of about 2700 B.C. with a ladder-mast which has been lowered on to a rest or crutch. Notice the thick rope or hogging-truss which runs from prow to stern to support the ship

At first the Egyptian ships were driven by oars and rowed by thirty or more slaves. Then a large square sail was added for use when the wind was suitable. It was fixed to a *ladder-mast*, hanging from a spar, later called a *yard*. Sailing ships eighty feet long were in use on the River Nile in 4000 B.C.

The trade routes of Egypt extended along 800 miles of the River Nile and by canal to the Red Sea. By 3000 B.C., Egyptian traders were sailing across the Mediterranean Sea to the island of Crete and the coast of Phoenicia. Travel by sea had begun.

Pictures carved on the walls of ancient temples tell us what the Egyptian ships were like, and provide details of certain voyages. A famous series of carvings describes a voyage down the Red Sea to Punt, which was probably the country now called Somaliland.

In 1500 B.C., Queen Hatshepsut sent ships there to obtain supplies of a gum called myrrh which was used as a perfume and as incense.

The ships took grain, pottery and papyrus to Punt and returned with rich cargoes of myrrh, rare woods, ivory, ebony, gold, panther skins and live apes.

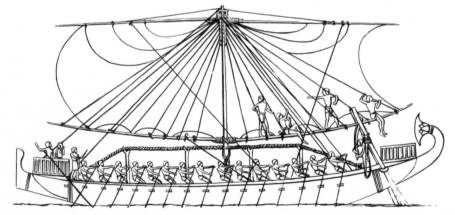

One of Queen Hatshepsut's sailing ships. Ropes called shrouds are used to hold the mast in position. The two steering paddles are turned by means of a tiller. The man in the bows is sounding the depth of the water

A Phoenician ship with a long keel which could be used to ram an enemy ship

3. PHOENICIAN SEAMEN

At this time, the Phoenicians were also learning how profitable it was to trade by sea. Their home was a narrow strip of land on the eastern shores of the Mediterranean where there was little room to herd animals or grow food. But they had two fine seaports named Tyre and Sidon. So they set out to become pedlars of the sea.

Unlike the Egyptians, the Phoenicians were too busy trading to make many pictures of their ships. But sometimes ships were depicted on coins. Some of these coins have been found at Sidon.

Obtaining wood from tall trees growing in Syria, the Phoenicians gave their ships proper keels. They made the keel stick out below the

bow to form a ram for use against enemy ships.

The Phoenician ship was fitted with square sails but was driven chiefly by oars. There were two or more banks of oars, one above the other.

Phoenicians building a ship

9

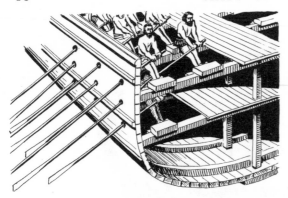

A possible position of rowers in a trireme

Types of ships were named according to the system of oars by which they were rowed. For a long time it was thought that these names referred to the number of banks of oars : that a ship with two banks was a *bi*reme (like *bi*cycle), three banks a *tri*reme (like *tri*cycle), four banks a *quad*rireme (like *quad*ruped), and five banks a *quin*quireme (like *quin*tet).

No one was certain how space was provided for the oarsmen. People wondered how long and heavy the oars would be in the top bank of a quinquireme.

In 1860 the Emperor of France, Napoleon III, had a *trireme* built from an ancient picture. It was found that the three banks of oars could be handled only with the greatest difficulty. Those of the top bank had to be almost twenty-five feet long to reach the water clear of those below. Their weight was such that several men were needed to pull them.

It was seen that a ship with five banks of oars was not practical. Perhaps the name quinquireme meant that five men pulled each oar.

In their ships the Phoenicians dared to sail to all parts of the Mediterranean and even through the Straits of Gibraltar to Britain. There they obtained tin from Cornwall in exchange for glassware, and linen dyed purple with a dye from shell-fish.

It was the Bronze Age and all the peoples of the Mediterranean world wanted tin. The Phoenicians would tell no one where the tin mines were. One captain, pursued by an enemy trying to discover the secret, purposely wrecked his ship so that the enemy ship, following close behind, was wrecked too.

Phoenician merchants

Some Phoenicians sailed as far north as the Baltic Sea to obtain amber. This was extremely valuable. It was used by the noble ladies of Rome for ornament and to dye their hair red ! The Phoenicians obtained so much gold for King Solomon of Israel that he no longer used any silver. Even his cups were made of gold.

About 600 B.C. the Pharaoh of Egypt sent a crew of Phoenicians out on a voyage of discovery. He told them to sail south from the Red Sea and try to find a way round to the Mediterranean.

It was three years before these sailors arrived

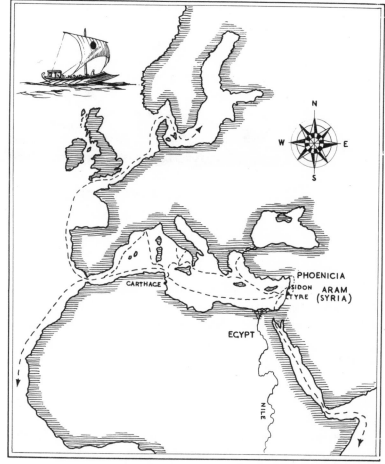

This map shows the voyages of the Phoenicians in the Mediterranean, round Africa, and to the Baltic Sea

back. They had sailed right round the continent of Africa, passing the Cape of Good Hope twenty centuries before it was rediscovered by Bartholomew Diaz !

The Phoenicians were probably the first sailors to use anchors. They used either a huge stone or a sack made from animal skin filled with stones.

Primitive anchors

A Greek warship

4. THE GREEKS

From about 1300 B.C. the Greeks began to sail in the Mediterranean. Their warships, fitted with a sail as well as oars, were shallow, open vessels which we call *galleys*. Like the Phoenician ships, they had rams.

These rams were used to good effect in the Battle of Salamis in 480 B.C. The Persians, who had overrun the East, sent an army to invade Greece, accompanied by a fleet including Phoenician ships, and numbering more than 1000 vessels.

As the mighty Persian fleet sailed towards Athens, the Persian ruler, Xerxes, had his throne set up on the nearby island of Salamis. There, from under a purple canopy, he watched the battle. He felt sure of victory. Instead, he saw his fleet wiped out by 300 Greek triremes.

The Greeks also had merchant ships. These were broader in width, or *beam*, than their warships and rose higher out of the water. They were driven by a single square sail, since rowers would have taken up space that could be used for cargo.

A Greek merchant ship

5. ROME AND CARTHAGE

In the meantime the city of Rome, in Italy, had been growing in power and was beginning to rival Carthage, on the coast of North Africa, a seaport founded by traders from Phoenicia. The Carthaginians were wealthy sea traders and brave sailors. In 520 B.C. a Carthaginian named Hanno had sailed 3000 miles along the west coast of Africa, returning to tell stories of a wild tribe of hairy men and women he had met. They were gorillas !

In 264 B.C. war broke out between Rome and Carthage. The Romans were not sea-faring people, but to match the sea-power of the Carthaginians they built a fleet of 160 ships in two months.

The Roman galleys were like the Greek ships but were more strongly built of fir and oak. They were copied from a Carthaginian ship captured after it had run aground.

The Romans invented a bridge for use in boarding enemy ships. This was called the *corvus*. On the end of the bridge was an iron spike which sank into the deck of the enemy ship, making the bridge fast. Then the Roman soldiers, the best-trained in the world, charged across.

13

Rivalry between Rome and Carthage finally ended in 146 B.C. when the Romans destroyed the enemy city. Then Roman galleys and merchant ships began to sail to all parts of the known world. Rome relied on her ships to bring food from other lands to feed her huge population.

A model of a Roman merchant ship

The Romans began to build broad, high ships to carry heavier cargoes. By A.D. 200 they were building ships 100 feet in length and 25 feet in the beam like the one shown here. They were as big as some ships in use fourteen centuries later.

At first they relied on a single square sail like the Greek merchant ships.

Later, one or two triangular topsails were placed above it. A second small mast, called an *artemon*, was pushed out over the bow and on this was set a square sail, smaller than the mainsail.

Then, at last, ships were able to do more than run before a following wind. They could use winds blowing at right angles to their course, which are called *beam winds*.

The Roman Empire stretched westwards to Britain. There, at the end of the third century A.D., the Romans were faced by new enemies. These were Saxon pirates who rowed long galleys across the North Sea to plunder the shores of Britain.

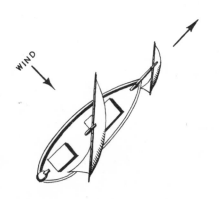

A beam wind

A Viking ship

6. NORSE LONGSHIPS

In A.D. 410 the Romans left Britain. During the next two centuries, fleet after fleet of Saxon sea rovers crossed the sea, first to plunder Britain and later to settle there. Then, in the eighth century, from Norway, Sweden and Denmark, came the Vikings or Norsemen, using similar war galleys. The Viking boats, long and narrow, were called *longships*. As remains have been found of more than thirty of them, we know exactly what they were like.

They were double-ended ; that is, their bow and stern were alike. This allowed them to sail ahead or astern, which was useful in the narrow fjords of their home waters. Bow and stern rose in a curve high out of the water, and the bow at

least was decorated with a dragon's head of fearsome appearance.

The longships were shallow enough to sail far up rivers, yet strong enough to weather fierce storms in the open sea. They carried a single square sail of brightly striped cloth on a mast about forty feet high. The chieftains were proud of their sails. Decorated sails were given to them by kings as a mark of honour.

The longships also carried oars which Viking warriors rowed standing up. There were about sixteen pairs of oars in a longship carrying a crew of ninety. When they were not in use, the holes for the oars were covered by wooden shutters. The warriors hung their shields over the gunwale, ready for use, and to protect themselves from wind and spray.

Leif Ericsson's ship in Arctic waters

The Vikings were skilled sailors as well as fierce warriors. They discovered Iceland in A.D. 861, and Greenland in 982. In A.D. 1000 Leif Ericsson sailed from Greenland to a place he called Vinland, which was probably Nova Scotia. So Ericsson discovered America five centuries before Christopher Columbus reached the West Indies.

As the longships were open boats with no decks, a tent was put up amidships in rough weather to provide shelter.

It was the custom of the Vikings to bury a chieftain in his ship. The ship was carried ashore and the chief's body was placed in it, together with his arms and other possessions. Then a mound of earth and stones was built over the vessel.

It is in such mounds that longships have been found. At Gokstad, in Norway, a Viking ship was discovered and is now in a museum at Oslo. It measures 76 feet 7 inches long and 17 feet 6 inches in the beam.

A Viking ship-burial

This Viking ship was discovered at Gokstad in Norway

In 1892 a copy of this ship was made, and twelve men sailed it across the Atlantic Ocean. They made the voyage to America in less than four weeks.

The Viking ships were fitted with a rudder in the form of a large, wide

The figurehead of a Norse ship

B

oar on the right-hand side. The earliest ships had used two steering oars, one at each side, and as late as the second century Roman merchant vessels still used two oars.

Stern with steering oar

The single steering oar was first used in the Mediterranean. As the people of the East believed that the right eye and the right side of the body were stronger than the left, it was placed on the right-hand side of the ship, giving it the name of *starboard* (from steerboard). This side was always kept clear of the shore when mooring so that the oar would not be damaged. Because of this the left-hand side of the ship became known as the *port* side.

A sea-battle between Saxon and Viking ships

7. ALFRED'S NAVY

In A.D. 886, Alfred the Great, King of Wessex, was fighting the Danes. He knew that he could never defeat them unless he could drive them back at sea. So he had ships built " well-nigh twice as long as the others. Some had sixty oars, some had more. They were both swifter and also higher than the others."

They were not shaped like the Viking longships but " as it seemed to himself that they might be more useful ". What this shape was, we do not know, but we do know that Alfred's ships had rams.

They made up the first English navy. Our Royal Navy of today is descended from it.

But the English Navy was not kept strong. Canute became king of England in 1016. He had no use for a strong navy because he ruled an Empire that stretched from Denmark to England. So there were few ships to oppose William, Duke of Normandy, when he invaded England in 1066, and these had been withdrawn to the Thames when Harold dispersed his anti-invasion troops.

Part of the Bayeux Tapestry, embroidered by Norman ladies, which tells the story of the invading fleet of William the Conqueror. Here the Normans are setting sail for England with their horses on board

8. THE NORMAN FLEET

William the Conqueror had a fleet of transports built to carry his army of 10–12,000 men with some cavalry horses across the Channel. William himself was the grandson of a Viking pirate and he built ships that were like the Viking longships. They relied upon sails and the invasion had to wait until a favourable wind blew.

In the centuries that followed the Norman Conquest, ships of the West developed from those of the Norsemen. In 1078 William the Conqueror ordered the towns of Sandwich, Dover, Hythe, Romney and Hastings to supply fighting ships for the Crown. They were given the name of Cinque Ports, which means Five Ports, and they keep that name today. It is from the seals of the Cinque Ports that we know what ships looked like in the following centuries.

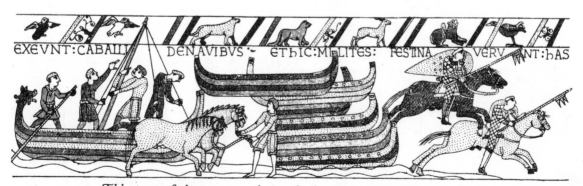

This part of the tapestry shows the landing of the Norman ships at Pevensey near Hastings

9. THE CASTLED SHIP

The seal of Sandwich

This seal of Sandwich dated 1238 shows a double-ended ship with raised platforms fitted with battlements at bow and stern. Bowmen and soldiers stood on these platforms during a battle.

The platforms were called the *forecastle* and the *aftercastle*. The forward part of a merchant ship is still called the *forecastle* (pronounced *fo'c's'le*).

As ships were built bigger they had to rely more and more upon their sails to drive them. The sailors of the West became skilled in handling sails, and learned how to reduce the sail area by tying, or reefing, the sails for safety in bad weather.

Ships driven by oars must ride high in the water so that the rowers pull the ship *over* the water rather than

through it. This kind of vessel is said to be " of shallow draught ". Sail-driven ships could be of deeper draught. Instead of being open, these ships were covered in with a deck. The platforms at bow and stern gave them the name *castled ships*.

In the thirteenth century, for the first time, someone had the idea of steering the ship from over the stern instead of from the side. So the steering oar became the *rudder*.

A stern rudder

After this, the stern of the ship was made to rise from the water as straight as possible for the rudder to be fitted on to it. The last traces of the double-ended ship began to vanish.

Projecting from the bow was the *bowsprit*. It was like the Roman artemon, but it had a different use. Lines were made fast to the end of it from the edges of the front sail, so that the ship could sail closer into the wind.

A bowsprit

10. IN THE MEDITERRANEAN

The ships of the Mediterranean were being developed with ideas which came from the East. In the seventh century they had adopted the triangular or *lateen* sail. This was first used on Arab ships in the Indian Ocean.

The lateen sail was set along the length of the ship (i.e., *fore and aft*), instead of across it like the square sail. It is better than a square sail when a beam wind is blowing. Some Mediterranean ships began to carry lateen sails on two masts or even on three. Arab *dhows* still use lateen sails.

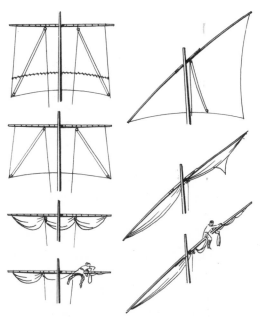

Reefing a square sail and a lateen sail

Arab dhows on the River Nile today

The sea-battle between Richard I's fleet and the Moslem dromon

11. CRUSADERS' SHIPS

In 1191 Richard the Lionheart sailed for the Holy Land with a fleet of 200 ships in the Third Crusade. Off the coast of Syria they came upon a massive vessel fitted with oars and lateen sails on three masts. It was a Moslem warship called a *dromon*.

The hull of the dromon was completely covered with green and yellow leather. It towered like a giant over Richard's little single-masted ships and galleys. Catapults on the dromon opened fire on the Christian fleet with glass balls containing a burning liquid called " Greek fire ". But the dromon was finally rammed and sunk. Crusaders said afterwards that there were 1500 men aboard.

While the Crusades continued, sea traffic in the Mediterranean was heavy. It was mostly in the hands of three Italian cities, Venice, Genoa and Pisa. They sent merchant ships with supplies for the Crusaders, and brought back from captured ports in Syria cargoes of goods that had come overland from the Far East.

The Italian merchant ship was a descendant of the Roman. In the twelfth century it was still a tubby vessel with a single lateen sail. But by the fifteenth century it had grown into the *carrack*.

A carrack of the fifteenth century

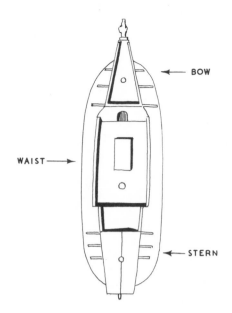

Plan of a carrack

12. CARRACK AND CARAVEL

Like the Moslem ships, the carrack had three masts. The mainmast carried a large square sail; the foremast carried a smaller square sail; and the mast at the rear, which was given the Arab name of *mizzen*, carried a lateen sail.

Like the ships of the West, the carrack was castled. But its forecastle and aftercastle (sometimes called a *summer-castle*) were built as part of the ship instead of being added on to it. As a result, the deck was in three pieces—bow, waist and stern. The waist was the lowest part of the deck, and the cargo was stored there. A carrack might be 125 feet long and 34 feet wide.

Carracks began to be used in the West as well as in the Mediterranean.

The caravel was a smaller and more graceful type of carrack. At first it was lateen-rigged, but later square sails were fitted to the foremast.

A caravel

DIRECTION OF WIND

DIRECTION OF PROGRESS ⟶

How a ship tacks to sail into a head wind

In such ships as these, sailors learned to use the wind to the best advantage. Indeed they found that by *tacking* they could sail into a wind. Longer voyages became possible.

Caravels were the ships which were used when Henry the Navigator's sailors made the first great voyages of discovery.

Carracks from Venice and Genoa carried rich cargoes across the Mediterranean from the East. They brought jewels, gold, ivory and spices. Of these, the spices were the most valuable. It was said that a peck of pepper was worth more than a man's life.

People wanted spices to make their food more tasty. So, from the Indies and the Far East, pepper, ginger, cinnamon, nutmeg and other spices were carried to the Middle East by ship across the Indian Ocean or overland by caravan.

In the fourteenth century the ports of Syria were captured by the Turks. The trade routes to the East were almost closed. Only the ships of Venice were able to obtain spices by way of Alexandria, in Egypt.

PART TWO: THE AGE OF DISCOVERY

13. PRINCE HENRY THE NAVIGATOR

People began to look for a new way to the East. As early as 1410, Henry the Navigator, Prince of Portugal, had this in mind. His idea was to bring spices from the Indies in Portuguese ships sailing round Africa. In a lonely observatory at Sagres, on the shores of the Atlantic Ocean, Prince Henry made his plans. He studied maps and old documents; he drew up plans for ships; he taught sailors how to steer their ships in the open sea. Then he sent them to find a way round Africa to the Indian Ocean.

The Portuguese ships were usually caravels. They carried a square foresail with lateens on two or three other masts. For long voyages this arrangement of sails had been found

The world as it was known at the beginning of the fifteenth century

better than lateen sails alone. It allowed full use to be made of any following wind.

In such a caravel, in 1434, Captain Gil Eannes sailed past Cape Bojador on the west coast of Africa. Sailors had feared that beyond this point lay the edge of the earth, for they thought that the world was shaped like a saucer.

Henry the Navigator died in 1460, twenty-seven years before the southern tip of Africa was turned by Bartholomew Diaz with two tiny caravels. Diaz called the headland where the coast turned eastwards the Cape of Storms. King John II of Portugal changed the name to the Cape of Good Hope, for it provided hope of a new route to the East.

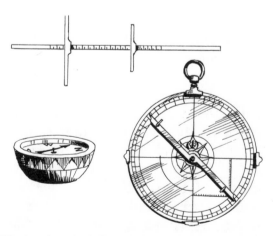

Navigational instruments of the fifteenth century: a cross-staff, a compass and an astrolabe

Christopher Columbus reaches the West Indies

14. THE SHIPS OF COLUMBUS

Christopher Columbus, a sailor from Genoa, believed that the world was round like a ball. This meant, he said, that the East could be reached by ships sailing westwards.

No one took any notice of Columbus for a long time. Then King Ferdinand of Spain gave him three ships to test his idea : the *Niña*, the *Pinta* and the *Santa Maria*.

They were three tiny vessels to face the task of crossing the Atlantic Ocean. The *Santa Maria* was a carrack ; the *Niña* and the *Pinta* were caravels only half her size.

No one knows for sure what these ships looked like. No pictures of them have been found. But we know from notes what they probably looked like.

The *Santa Maria* was a decked ship with three masts. Her mainmast carried, beside the mainsail, a smaller square sail above it—a *topsail*. The foresail was square, the mizzen lateen. Probably she also had a small square sail fitted to her bowsprit—a *spritsail*. Spritsails came into use in the fifteenth century. The *Santa Maria* was probably 95 feet long and 25 feet in the beam, being smaller than a modern steam trawler. She carried a crew of fifty-two under Vice-Admiral Columbus. The *Pinta* was a three-masted caravel with square sails. The *Niña*, the smallest of the ships, was also a three-masted caravel. She started the voyage with lateen sails but they were later changed to square sails. Each caravel carried a crew of eighteen.

Columbus reached the West Indies in sixty-nine days. Then the *Santa Maria* was wrecked off the island of Santo Domingo. So Columbus built a fort with timber from the wreck, and, leaving twenty-five men to guard it, sailed back to Spain in the *Niña*.

He took with him spices, gold,

Christopher Columbus

strange animals, birds, and ten Indians as proof of his success. Columbus believed he had found a new way to the East. Instead, he had found a rich New World.

This reconstruction of the " Santa Maria " was made for a film

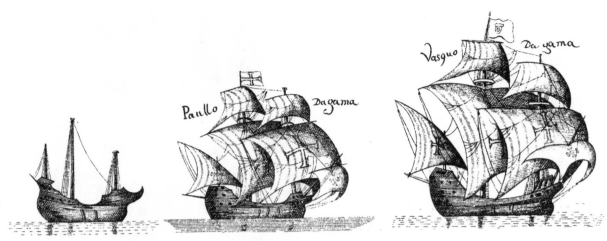

Three of Vasco da Gama's ships, including his flagship, " Sao Gabriel "

15. THE SEA ROUTE TO INDIA

In 1497 Vasco da Gama finally opened the trade route to the East by way of the Cape of Good Hope for Portugal. He sailed to Calicut, in India, with a fleet of four ships which included two carracks each more than twice as big as the *Santa Maria*. Da Gama reached Calicut after eleven months and he returned to Portugal with a rich cargo of spices. The voyages of Columbus and Vasco Da Gama were the most important since men first put to sea in ships. They extended the sea trading routes of the world for the first time in sixteen centuries. They also made Spain and Portugal the leading nations on the seas.

Bigger and bigger carracks were built for use on the new trade routes. They carried fabulous cargoes home to the ports of Spain and Portugal.

As their power grew, Spain and Portugal were in danger of becoming enemies. So Pope Alexander VI drew an imaginary line down the middle of the Atlantic Ocean. All lands discovered to the east of this line would be Portugal's, he said ; all lands discovered to the west, Spain's. The two countries agreed to this.

At the same time, other countries were growing jealous of the wealth and power of Spain and Portugal. Sailors from England, France and Holland set out to discover new sea routes and new lands for their countries.

The Battle of Lepanto, 1571

16. THE GALLEASS

The spread of the Turkish Empire had already reduced the power of Venice and Genoa. In 1517 the Turks conquered Egypt and the last of the old trade routes to the East was closed to Christians. Venice became engaged in a bitter struggle with the Turks which reached a climax in 1571. Then the Turks were beaten in the Battle of Lepanto by the combined forces of Venice, Genoa, Pisa and Spain.

In this battle Venice used a new fighting ship—the *galleass*, a heavier form of galley with three lateen sails. Lepanto was the last naval battle in which oared ships played an important part, the galleasses of Venice saving Europe from being overrun by the Turks.

Venetian noblemen who commanded galleasses had great faith in these vessels. They swore on their honour never to refuse battle even against twenty-five enemy galleys !

A Venetian galleass

Mediterranean galleys in about 1560

17. MEDITERRANEAN GALLEYS

As a result of the improvement in sailing ships, galleasses were little used after the seventeenth century. Yet the galley continued to be used in the Mediterranean for another two hundred years. It was a favourite craft of the Barbary pirates.

Like the galley of old, it was long and narrow and rose no more than four feet from the water.

There was usually one mast forward, carrying a lateen sail, and the bow ended in a ram.

On an open deck sat two rows of oarsmen. Between them ran a raised platform along which the overseer strode with his long whip.

The galleys were rowed by slaves or convicts. A fit galley slave was worth £8 10s. 0d. For stealing, a man might be sent to the galleys for ten years.

A fit man could pull an oar at top speed for only an hour, but galley captains sometimes tried to travel fast for much longer. Then, to keep up the strength of the rowers, bread soaked in wine was put into their mouths. If a slave failed to keep the pace, he was whipped. If he still failed, he was thrown overboard as a warning to the others.

The " Matthew " returning in triumph to Bristol

18. REBUILDING THE NAVY: JOHN CABOT'S VOYAGE

In 1490 King Henry VII began to rebuild the English Navy. In that year the *Regent* was launched. She was a four-masted warship, a form of carrack, 80 feet long and 30 feet in the beam. The foremast and the mainmast carried square sails; the mizzen and a fourth mast, which was called the *bonaventure mizzen*, carried lateens.

The *Regent* had no aftercastle but rose at the stern in a high *poop*. She carried 225 little cannon, firing balls weighing one pound. These were too small to damage the hull of an enemy vessel, but they were aimed at the sails and the rigging.

The news of Columbus' first voyage to the West Indies caused Henry VII to turn his attention to merchant shipping. In 1497 he sent John Cabot, an Italian sailor who had settled in Bristol, out into the Atlantic Ocean in a little carrack named the *Matthew*. Cabot reached Newfoundland and claimed that country for England.

Upon his return he was greeted as a hero at his home port of Bristol. He also received a reward from the King for claiming England's first land in the New World. Henry was well-known for being careful with money, and the reward was a gift of £10 !

A merchant ship of the sixteenth century

19. THE " GREAT HARRY "

Henry VIII carried on the work of rebuilding the Navy. He added eighty ships to it, including the famous warship *Henri Grâce à Dieu* or *Great Harry*. Remains of the *Great Harry* were found in the mud of the River Thames in 1812. They showed her to have been a strong, heavy vessel built of oak.

She was a tall ship 180 feet long and six times as big as the *Santa Maria*. She had a high poop, square at the stern, which contained three decks. She carried 230 small cannon and 21 large cannon. These were able to fire balls weighing 60 lb. apiece. The combined fire of port or starboard guns was called a *broadside*.

The *Great Harry* made a wonderful picture on state occasions. The oak hull of the ship was oiled black and the upperworks were painted in bright colours. Her sails were made from cloth of gold and she carried twenty-eight banners of silk, decorated with gold and silver, ten flags of St. George and seven other banners.

No prouder ship ever floated. She cost £8708 5s. 3d. to build—an enormous sum in those days. Yet she was never tested in a sea battle. She was destroyed by fire in 1553 when at anchor in the Thames.

Ships such as the *Great Harry* were called *great ships*. Like the carrack, the great ship had a very broad hull; the *Great Harry*, 180 feet long, was probably as much as 50 feet in the beam.

20. THE GALLEON

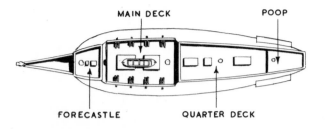

The deck plan of a galleon

In the reign of Queen Elizabeth I, the *great ship* gave way to the *galleon*. The galleon's hull was more slender than the carrack's, and she lay lower in the water.

It was in a galleon that Francis Drake became the first Englishman to sail round the world.

England's galleons were never longer than 150 feet. They sailed faster and could change direction more easily than the great ship or carrack. The galleon still rose at bows and stern, but much less than the great ship. Her bow ended in a beak sticking out from the hull, usually decorated with some ornament such as a dragon or a fantastic animal with the body of a snake. This was the ship's *figurehead*.

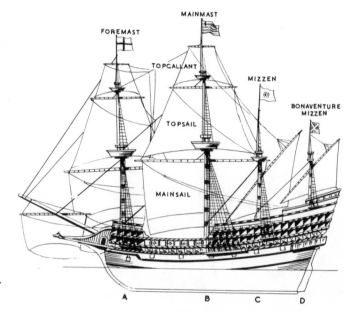

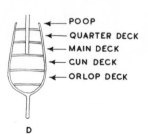

The sail plan and cross-sections of the hull of an Elizabethan galleon

" Vittoria ", the first ship to sail round the world. The artist has translated the ship's name

The first voyage round the world had been made by a two-masted carrack in the service of Spain, the *Vittoria*. With four other ships in a fleet commanded by Ferdinand Magellan, the *Vittoria* sailed from Seville in August 1519. The fleet made its way south-westwards, sailed along the east coast of South America, passed through the Strait of Magellan and reached the Pacific Ocean by this new sea-passage. After an absence of three years the *Vittoria* returned alone with Sebastian del Cano in command, Magellan having been killed by natives in the Philippine Islands.

Drake checks the course of his ships

Francis Drake's galleon was named *Pelican* when she sailed from Plymouth in 1577. She was smaller than the *Santa Maria*—75 feet long and about 20 feet in the beam. Her foremast and mainmast carried two square sails and her mizzen carried a lateen.

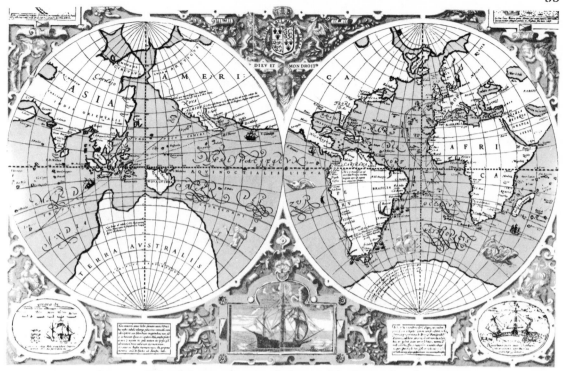

A map of Drake's voyage round the world, drawn in about 1590

Four smaller ships set out with the *Pelican*, but two were destroyed and two turned back. Drake changed the name of his ship to the *Golden Hind* when she reached the Strait of Magellan leading from the Atlantic into the Pacific Ocean. Drake sailed along the west coast of South America. As he went, he attacked and plundered Spanish treasure ships and Spanish ports. Then the *Golden Hind* sailed westwards across the Pacific Ocean.

The " Golden Hind "

Upon Drake's return to England after a voyage lasting almost three years, Queen Elizabeth went aboard the *Golden Hind* and knighted him. His ship was placed on show in the Thames, where she remained until 1670.

22. THE ARMADA SHIPS

Drake's kinsman, Sir John Hawkins, after a notable career as a sailor, was given the task of looking after the Navy. It was he who had galleons built to replace the clumsier *great ships* of Henry VIII.

Under Hawkins' direction, the masts, previously one long pole, were now made in sections (the mast, topmast, and topgallant mast). This meant that when a mast was broken, only the damaged section would have to be renewed, and not the whole mast.

Even though many new ships were built, the Navy had only thirty-four ships ready to face the Great Armada when it sailed against England in 1588. Merchant ships joined them to bring the English fleet to 197 ships. The biggest of these was the twenty-

The " Ark Royal "

seven-year-old great ship, *Triumph*, captained by Sir Martin Frobisher.

Lord Howard of Effingham, the commander of the English fleet, sailed in the *Ark Royal*, a four-masted galleon carrying three square sails on foremast and mainmast, two lateens on the mizzen and one lateen on the bonaventure. The new third square sail was called a *topgallant*. Drake sailed in the *Revenge*, a four-masted galleon armed with forty guns.

So big were the ships of the Armada, said one writer of those days, that " the ocean groaned beneath their weight ". But most of them were slow and difficult to handle. About one hundred and thirty Spanish ships sailed against England, of which thirty-seven were fighting-ships, the rest being troop transports and small craft. Less than half the great fleet ever returned to Spain.

A Spanish galleon

By defeating the Armada, England became a leading power on the seas. Holland was to become her chief rival. The Dutch had taken control of the trade route round South Africa to the Spice Islands. One result of this was that the price of pepper went up, becoming too dear for people in England to buy.

In 1600 the East India Company was formed in London, with permission from Queen Elizabeth I to trade between England and the East. The Company soon began to build their own ships at Deptford, on the Thames. People called them " East Indiamen ".

At first they were four-masters with three square sails on foremast and mainmast, and a lateen and a square topsail on mizzen and bonaventure. Later, in common with most vessels, East Indiamen became three-masters, the bonaventure being no longer used.

An early East Indiaman

and passengers could sleep undisturbed, they hove-to, arranging their sails to counteract one another and bring the ship to a standstill.

The East Indiaman was armed like a warship against attack by pirates or trade rivals. She was less graceful than the galleon, having low, blunt bows and a high stern. The stern curved up from the water-line before being squared off like a galleon's. This was known as the *round-tuck* stern. At first it was used only by English ships. Foreign ships continued to have square sterns, which were called *transoms*.

The round-tuck stern

These ships made no haste on their voyages between London and the East. At night, so that the captain

The transom

The " Mayflower " sets out for the New World

Meantime James I was strengthening the Navy. In 1610 the *Royal Prince* was launched, the largest ship up to that time. She was a three-master, 130 feet long and some 30 feet in the beam : the first British ship to have three covered gun decks. She carried two sails on her bowsprit—*spritsail* and *sprit topsail*.

But the most celebrated ship of this time was the *Mayflower*, a typical merchantman of the day, which carried the Pilgrim Fathers to America in 1620.

The *Royal Prince* was followed, twenty-seven years later, by the outstanding warship of the seventeenth century—Charles I's *Sovereign of the Seas*, a three-master, 232 feet long and 48 feet in the beam. She had three gun decks and carried 132 guns, and she was the first English warship to carry four sails on foremast and mainmast. All were square, the topmost sail being called a *royal*. The mizzen of the *Sovereign* carried a lateen below square topsail and topgallant.

The *Sovereign* was lavishly decorated with gilded wood carvings and other ornaments. This was the fashion of the times. So lavish had the decoration of ships become by 1703 that the Navy shipwrights were ordered to reduce it. After being cut

The gilded stern of the " Sovereign "

down to two decks in 1652, the *Sovereign* remained in service until she was sixty-two years old. Then she was destroyed by fire while being refitted at Chatham Docks.

The " Sovereign of the Seas "

In 1651, Oliver Cromwell, Lord Protector of the Commonwealth of England, brought in a law which stopped Dutch ships from bringing foreign cargoes to England. This led to a war from 1652 to 1654 in which Admiral Robert Blake, of England, and Admiral Van Tromp, of Holland, fought sea-battles in a new way.

They formed their ships into lines, one following the other, and tried to get into a position with the wind behind them when they faced the enemy fleet. Then they swept past the enemy, one by one, firing broadsides, with no danger of hitting friendly ships.

Van Tromp is said to have fastened a broom to his mast to show that he had swept the English from the sea. Blake fastened a whip to his to show that he was going to whip the Dutch from the waves. The Dutch were finally beaten. Van Tromp was killed.

The Navy Board inspecting the model of a new warship in 1651

Since the tiny ships of Prince Henry the Navigator first dared the open seas, two centuries had passed. In that time ships had grown to ten times the size of the *Santa Maria*.

By the seventeenth century, trade routes stretched round the world. Ships of all nations sailed the open seas for peaceful purposes. At the same time, strong navies were being built up.

Firing a broadside

24. LIFE IN SAILING SHIPS

In ancient times few passengers travelled by sea. When they did they were treated as members of a ship's crew and had to take their turn at the oars. A scholar who sailed from Asia Minor to Athens in 600 B.C. said afterwards : " There are three kinds of people—the living, the dead, and those at sea."

At the time of the Crusades, pilgrims to the Holy Land began to use ships to cross the Mediterranean instead of making the long overland journey. They had to sleep on deck or among the merchandise in the hold.

A pilgrim looks for somewhere to sleep

The fare was high and the pilgrims were so ill-treated on the voyage that the magistrates of Venice and Genoa made laws that a certain allowance of food and wine *had* to be given to travellers. Captains were also to allow a space of $5\frac{1}{2}$ feet by $1\frac{1}{2}$ feet between two people sleeping head to toe on deck !

By the fifteenth century it had become usual for the officers to have quarters in the stern and the men to share the forecastle. Often the men preferred remaining on the open deck to sleeping on bare boards in the cramped space of the fo'c's'le, overrun by vermin and full of the smell of bilge water from the hold below.

When, in Elizabethan times, someone suggested that England's gallant sea-dogs deserved better conditions aboard ship, Sir Walter Raleigh was among those who disagreed. He said that better conditions might make them grow soft !

Yet Drake had splendid quarters for himself and his officers when he sailed round the world. There were fine oak furniture, silver cutlery, and fiddlers to play while the officers dined.

The conditions under which the ordinary seaman lived produced a mental illness called " sailor's vapours ". This made men ill-tempered and vicious, and often led to quarrelling and fighting.

Sailors' quarters below deck

25. FOOD AT SEA

Many ships were infested by rats

Sailors' food consisted of hard biscuits, salt pork and sometimes dried peas or beans. Often the biscuits had weevils in them and the pork was rotten. The cook boiled the peas and beans to make a watery soup.

Cheese was sometimes carried but, in the tropics, it went bad and made men ill. In later times cows or goats were taken aboard to provide fresh milk. They were kept on deck and soon met with injury when a ship ran into bad weather. They were then killed and for a day or two the sailors had fresh meat to eat.

Occasionally chickens were kept in coops on the deck to provide eggs for the crew, but the decks were often awash and the luckless birds were drowned.

Beer and water were taken aboard and all the sailors drank beer for as long as it lasted. All the ship's water was carried in casks and no one could find a way to keep it fresh.

In a very short time it became brackish and covered with green slime.

Such poor food caused a disease called *scurvy*. As early as the seventeenth century it was known that fresh fruit and vegetables helped to prevent this. The Dutch set up stations on their trading routes where such food could be obtained. But other nations, including Britain, were not so concerned with the welfare of their sailors.

The hardships of sailors are shown in this extract from the journal of Magellan's voyage round the world : " We ate biscuits reduced to powder and full of grubs and we drank water that was yellow and stinking." They also ate leather, sawdust and rats. Two hundred and seventy men set out in Magellan's ships in 1519. Only eighteen, most of them weak and ailing, returned home in the *Vittoria* under Sebastian del Cano.

Milking cows on deck

PART THREE: THE GREAT DAYS OF SAIL

26. WARSHIPS OF THE EIGHTEENTH CENTURY

In the eighteenth century, warships were classed according to the number of guns they carried:

First rate	Three decks	100	guns
Second rate	Three decks	90	guns
Third rate	Two or three decks	60–80	guns
Fourth rate	Two decks	50–60	guns
Fifth rate	One deck	30–44	guns
Sixth rate	One deck	20–30	guns

Ships carrying fifty or more guns were classed as *ships of the line* because they sailed in the line which faced the enemy in battle. During the French wars of the eighteenth century the most popular size of battleship was the seventy-four-gunner.

The hull of an English warship was painted black with broad yellow bands between the rows of guns. The gun decks were painted red so that the bloodstains would not be noticed.

In 1756 the *Royal George* was launched, a three-decked vessel of a hundred guns, bigger and better-equipped than any battleship previously built in England. Some people called her a " floating gun battery ", but she was really a beautiful ship and the pride of the nation.

The " Royal George "

The *Royal George* was followed in 1765 by the most famous of all warships, the *Victory*, a ship of a hundred guns. The *Victory* was the flagship of Lord Nelson at the Battle of Trafalgar on October 21, 1805. That was the last great battle in which sailing ships took part. In it, the sea power of France was smashed.

42

Ships of many different kinds were being developed for different purposes in the eighteenth century. A few big ships began to carry four masts ; but three remained the usual number.

In the search for greater speed a new type of sail had come into use—the *studding sail*. Studding sails were little extra sails set on each side of the normal square sails, to catch the slightest breeze.

About 1658, for the first time, Dutch ships had been fitted with triangular sails fixed to the ropes supporting the masts. These sails, which ran fore and aft, were called *staysails*. When they were used on the foremast stays, they were called *jibs*. By 1712, such sails were being used on the smaller warships in place of the sprit sail.

Jibs were first carried on small boats in Holland called *jachts*. In 1660 the Dutch gave two of these little craft to Charles II who was a keen sailor.

Charles II's yacht

The *yachts*, as they were called in England, were rigged fore and aft. Their mainsail was fitted with a spar called a *gaff*, a development from the lateen sail.

Three-masted ships were losing their lateen mizzen. First of all, the part of the lateen sail in front of the mast was cut off, and finally, in about 1800, the yard was replaced by a gaff. This rose at an angle behind the mast. Forward, the yacht carried a staysail and a jib. It also carried a square topsail.

Royal yard

Topgallant yard

Top sail yard

Main yard.

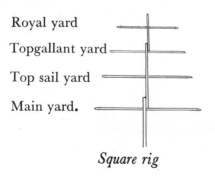

Square rig

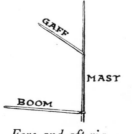

Fore-and-aft rig

H.M.S. " Victory ", Nelson's flagship

In the eighteenth century, warships began to use sails like the yacht's mainsail on their mizzens. In time this sail was extended over the stern, being fastened at the bottom to a boom which the Navy called a *driver*. Merchant sailors called it a *spanker*. Their ships began to carry this fore-and-aft rig as well as, or in place of, square rig. During the eighteenth century, many experiments were made with the rigging of sailing ships. By the nineteenth century there were several different types of rigging, as you can see in the drawings of these two pages.

CUTTER : *one mast rigged fore and aft ; broad-beamed hull*

SCHOONER : *two or more masts, fore-and-aft rigged*

BRIGANTINE : *two masts ; foremast square-rigged, mainmast rigged fore and aft*

BRIG : *two masts, both square-rigged*

BARQUENTINE : *rigged fore and aft on all masts except foremast*

BARQUE : *square-rigged on all masts save that nearest stern*

SLOOP : *one mast, rigged fore and aft ; therefore like a yacht*

LUGGER : *a two- or three-masted vessel using sails. These were square sails hung sideways from the masts*

Sailing ships were said to be *full-rigged* when they carried as many sails as possible. This might be as many as seven on each mast. The lowest sails were known, together, as the *courses* ; otherwise they were called *foresail*, *mainsail* and *cross-jack*.

The topsails were called *fore topsail*, *main topsail* and *mizzen topsail*. Some pirate ships to whom speed was all-important, are said to have had, above the *skysails*, extra sails called *moonrakers* !

7 Skysail

6 Royal

5 Upper topgallant

4 Lower topgallant

3 Upper topsail

2 Lower topsail

1 Mainsail

A full-rigged ship

In the Middle Ages sailors often shared in the profits of a voyage, and they did so still in the time of Drake. But with the development of the big trading companies in the seventeenth and eighteenth century, the adventurous sea-dog gave way to the ordinary seaman.

Before, sailors had endured strict discipline and poor conditions with the prospect of a rich reward in mind, but now only the meanest people took to the sea.

Indeed, some men had to be tricked or trapped into going to sea.

Conditions in ships of the Royal Navy were even worse than those in merchant ships. Dishonest dealers supplied food that was short in weight or bad, perhaps bribing an officer to overlook this. The sailors

Flogging a sailor with a " cat-o'-nine-tails "

suffered in silence or growled among themselves. They were afraid to complain.

Discipline aboard ships was strict. Flogging was a common punishment, perhaps sixty lashes with the cat-o'-nine-tails. But it must be remembered that many of the seamen were desperadoes and gaol-birds who would not hesitate to mutiny and turn pirate if the opportunity arose.

Discipline at sea has always been strict because the dangers are great. During his voyage round the world, Drake had one of his own friends, Sir Thomas Doughty, executed, because he was accused of plotting against his Admiral. The captain of a ship at sea demands perfect obedience.

Sometimes sailors rebelled against the harsh discipline. In 1789 Captain Bligh of the *Bounty* was set adrift by his crew in one famous mutiny.

Captain Bligh is set adrift by the mutineers

A sailor is seized by the Press Gang

Some men preferred dying on the scaffold to being sent to sea. This was a time when magistrates were told to send criminals into the Navy instead of to prison. Dr. Johnson said : " Being in a ship is being in a jail, with the chance of being drowned."

29. THE PRESS GANG

The rulers of England had an ancient right to " press " men into the service of the Crown. So Press Gangs were sent out to seize men for service in the Navy.

One naval gunner wrote of the seaman's lot :

" A poor sailor has arrived home from a long voyage exulting in the pleasure of being among his dearest friends and relations. Behold him just entering the door when a press gang seizes him like a felon, drags him away and puts him into a tender's hold, and from thence he is sent aboard a man-o'-war perhaps ready to sail for some foreign station, without either seeing his wife, friends or relations ; if he complains, he is likely to be seized up and flogged with a cat, and if he deserts he is flogged round the fleet nearly to death. Surely they had better shoot a man at once."

The Press Gangs were at their most active during the Napoleonic Wars. One crew in 1805, for example, contained 15 farmers, 6 printers, 6 hatters, 4 spinners, 3 pedlars, 1 optician, 1 umbrella maker and 1 violin maker. These were some of the men who fought and won so gloriously at Trafalgar.

A sailor in the Napoleonic Wars

Once on board a ship, sailors were kept hard at work. The older *able seamen* looked after the lower rigging ; the younger *prime seamen* looked after the rigging aloft and were called *topmen*.

It was an officer's duty to keep the men busy at all times. An old, seaman's rhyme says :

" Six days shalt thou labour and
    do all thou art able,
And on the seventh—holystone
    the decks and scrape the cable."

Topmen reef the sails

30. MIDSHIPMEN

Boys aged no more than eleven were carried in some ships as cabin boys. After a few years at sea they were classed as *midshipmen*.

The midshipmen shared a tiny cabin on a deck below the water-line, close to the surgeon's cockpit. There they lived, ate, and slept in hammocks for which they were allowed fourteen inches of space each.

For an hour or two each day they had lessons from the ship's schoolmaster or the chaplain. They studied so that, when they were twenty, they could sit for the officer's examination.

Beside the boy midshipmen, there were others called *oldsters*. These were men who had failed to pass the officer's examination. The midshipmen had many jobs to do, such as seeing that sailors lashed their hammocks properly and supervising the men at work on the masts. The youngest of them could order a seaman to be flogged. They had to be saluted like officers, and one captain said, " Every man on this ship must salute a midshipman's coat, even if it's only hanging on a broomstick to dry."

The boys themselves could be punished, though not by flogging. They were often *mastheaded* ; that is, sent up to the main topmast crosstrees 150 feet above the deck.

Pirate ships attacking a merchant ship

31. "SAIL AHOY!"

Apart from the dangers of the sea itself, there was danger from rival traders and pirates. Here is an extract from a diary kept by a boy sailing in a merchant ship from Salem, Massachusetts, to Gibraltar, in 1759.

Nov. 12.   Saw a sail to the south-west. We fired a shot and she hoisted Dutch colours.

Nov. 15.   Between two and three this morning we saw two sail which chased us. One ship fired three shots at us which we returned. She proved to be the ship *Cornwall* from Bristol.

Nov. 23.   We now began to approach land. At eight o'clock, two Barbary pirate boats came out after us. They fired at us which we returned as merrily. They were glad to get away as well as they could. We stood after one,

but it was almost impossible to come up with the piratical dogs.

Dec. 10.   In the morning we heard firing. There was a vessel attacked by three of the piratical Teriffa boats. Two cutters in the government service soon got under sail.

(The ship being attacked had struck her colours, but the cutters rescued her and captured some of the pirates.)

The Barbary pirates or *Corsairs* had their headquarters along the coast of Algeria. Their activities continued until the French occupied Algeria in 1832.

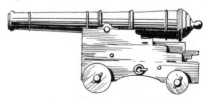

A ship's gun of the eighteenth century

In waters closer to home, ships had other enemies—the wreckers. People in coastal villages looked upon a wreck as a gift from heaven. They even prayed, " Please God, send us a wreck."

They fell upon any ship that was driven ashore and stripped it of everything. Sometimes the crew stayed aboard a wrecked ship in the hope of refloating her in fair weather. Then there would be a fight between sailors and villagers which usually ended with the crew being thrown overboard, to swim to safety if they could.

Looting a wrecked ship

32. THE END OF SCURVY

During the seventeenth and early eighteenth centuries, scurvy was one of the worst enemies of a sailor. It was not unusual for at least one-third of a ship's crew to die during a long voyage. Even close to land, disease was common. When our ships returned after chasing the Armada, more men died from disease than battle wounds. The only remedy at the time was to *purge* the ship by burning sulphur, and swab the decks and timbers with vinegar.

When, in 1740, Lord Anson sailed from England with eight ships to plunder Spanish vessels in the Pacific, his supplies were found to be bad from the start. One officer wrote that the biscuits were " scarce anything but dust ". The beef and pork were rotten, and " the surgeon endeavoured to hinder us from eating it, alleging that it was, tho' a slow, yet a sure poison ".

By the time the fleet reached Brazil, scurvy had already broken out and eighty men had to be put ashore to rest. After that, " we gave our ship a thorough cleaning ; then we smoked it between decks and after all washed every part well with vinegar. These operations were extremely necessary for correcting the noisome stench on board, and destroying the vermin."

By the time the Pacific was reached, 292 men in Anson's ship, the *Centurion*, had died of scurvy. The other ships in his fleet, now reduced to four, had also suffered and almost all the remaining men were sick. They spent 104 days resting on an island before they were fit to carry on.

On his three historic voyages of discovery in the Pacific, Captain Cook showed that such suffering could be avoided. When he sailed round the world with the *Resolution* and the *Adventure* in 1772-75 Cook lost only one man through scurvy.

Captain Cook

To prevent scurvy, his rations included lemons, conserved carrots, and the juice of herbs. Rations of salt beef and pork were reduced, and salt, butter and cheese were forbidden. Wild celery was gathered on Tierra del Fuego to provide a fresh vegetable and keep the dreaded disease away. As a result, Cook's men kept fit even during the longest voyages.

At first, the sailors did not like Cook's ideas, which meant keeping the ships spotlessly clean and taking the strange food. He never allowed a seaman to appear dirty before him, but inspected the men and their clothing every week.

Between decks, the ship was constantly " cured with fires " and " smoked with gunpowder mixed with vinegar "—which acted as a disinfectant. To the men, this seemed a lot of unnecessary trouble ; but in the end they loved their commander and looked upon him as a father.

It was partly owing to his example that, in 1795, the Royal Navy began to issue sailors with a daily ration of lime juice and lemon juice. Then they stopped suffering from scurvy.

The owners of merchant ships were not so worried about the health of their crews. But finally a law was passed making them follow the Navy's lead.

The U.S. frigate " Constitution " is chased by a British squadron

33. THE RISE OF THE FRIGATE

In the early years of the nineteenth century, although the first steamships were being successfully tried out on canals and rivers, there was still a long life ahead for the sailing-ship in trade and war.

During this period, American shipyards produced fast three-masted warships known as frigates. They were slender hulled, with four light sails to each mast. Some of them were fitted with 50 or 60 guns, which meant having an additional deck. In the naval war with the U.S.A. from 1812 to 1815, American frigates surprised the Royal Navy by their speed and powerful gunfire.

On August 19, 1812, for instance, the U.S. frigate *Constitution* met the British *Guerrière* off the coast of America. After thirty minutes the *Guerrière* surrendered. Later, the *Constitution* was chased for three days by a British squadron but managed to escape.

In the autumn and winter of 1812, five hundred British ships were run down and captured by the faster vessels of the enemy.

34. A VOYAGE TO INDIA

This account of a voyage to India gives a picture of the delays and dangers at sea just over a century ago.

On October 14, 1829, the *Lady Holland* sailed from Portsmouth to India. She was carrying a cargo worth £48,000 and twenty-two passengers, including Mr. and Mrs. Alexander Duff. Mr. Duff was a missionary of the Church of Scotland. He and his wife had been aboard the *Lady Holland* for eight days before a suitable wind blew to carry her into the Channel.

Just past the Isle of Wight the ship ran into a storm. The weather in the Bay of Biscay was not bad, but the winds were unfavourable and it was November 7 before the ship dropped anchor at Madeira alongside three frigates of the Royal Navy. A cargo of wine was being picked up at Madeira and the *Lady Holland* was to spend a week there. On the night before she was due to sail a ball was held ashore for her passengers and the officers of the frigates.

During the ball a gale arose. Every ship in the harbour was driven out to sea. Then three were driven back on shore and dashed to pieces. The others vanished into the night. It was three weeks before the *Lady*

On board the " Lady Holland " in calm weather

Holland was brought back to Madeira by the men who had remained on board her. At last, on December 3, she set sail for Cape Town. A frigate sailed with her through the pirate waters off the coast of North Africa and chased off one pirate ship.

Gales drove the *Lady Holland* westwards of her course as she headed for the Cape of Good Hope. Once she was close to the coast of Brazil. When she came to the Cape, she was driven past it three times.

Caught in a gale

The " Lady Holland " is wrecked

On February 13, 1830, two months after leaving Madeira and nearly four out from England, the *Lady Holland* was at last heading into Table Bay. But at ten o'clock that night, when most passengers were in their hammocks, a shock ran through the ship.

" Oh, she's gone, she's gone ! " cried a voice as some of them ran on deck. The ship had struck a reef and her back was broken.

The passengers, most of them wrapped in blankets, gathered in the main cabin in the stern. The captain and his crew cut down the masts to reduce the strain of the wind.

Mountainous seas were breaking on the reef but three seamen put off in a small boat to look for a landing place. After three long hours they returned, soaked and weary, but with good news. They had found a break in the reef.

The lifeboat was launched and, after several journeys, passengers and crew were landed on a small island from which they were later rescued and taken to Cape Town.

When the next East Indiamen called there, the passengers from the *Lady Holland* tried to obtain places aboard, but the ships were full. It was March before Mr. and Mrs. Duff found berths aboard the *Moira*, paying £260 in gold for them.

The *Moira* was soon driven off course by gales and ran into a hurricane off Mauritius. It was the end of May before she dropped anchor at the mouth of the Ganges in India.

Still the Duffs' troubles were not over. A cyclone struck the ship and she was lifted on to a muddy island. Stranded on her side, the *Moira* had to be abandoned. Passengers and crew struggled ashore in driving rain and howling wind.

News of the wreck reached Calcutta and a fleet of small boats came down the river Hooghli to their aid. In one of them Mr. and Mrs. Alexander Duff reached Calcutta on May 27, 1830, almost eight months after they had left England.

A clipper carrying tea from China

35. THE COMING OF THE CLIPPER

The shipbuilders who produced the graceful frigates of the war of 1812 also produced a series of fast little merchant ships. Then they designed a big ship for fast sailing, called the *clipper*. The first of these, the *Ann McKim*, was built in Baltimore in 1832.

The days when merchant ships need not hurry were coming to an end. Since the seventeenth century, certain companies had kept for themselves the right of trading in certain ports. But in 1833, the last of the East India Company's agreements for trading in the East came to an end. After that, trade was open to all.

The clipper was a three-masted ship with a low, slender hull, six times as long as it was broad in the beam, and a bow that was sharp and narrow. She carried a vast area of sail in all weathers, perhaps five sails on each mast, a mass of stay-sails, and studding sails as well. Under full sail she was a beautiful sight.

In 1849 the clipper *Oriental* caused a sensation by carrying a cargo of tea from Hong Kong to London in the record time of ninety-seven days. Tea loses its flavour rapidly. So it was important to deliver it quickly in those days, when it was not packed in sealed chests as it is now. "Yankee" clippers began to steal the trade in tea from the slower English ships.

English ships continued to lose trade until a Liverpool shipowner had an idea. He ordered four clippers from the U.S.A.

Then English shipbuilders began to produce clippers. In 1850 *Challenger* was launched. She raced the U.S. clipper *Challenge* from China and beat her.

36. THE TEA RACES

The start of the Civil War in the U.S.A. in 1861 ended the rivalry between the U.S. and Great Britain. But rivalry continued between companies and ships. The delivery of the first tea crop in London became a great sporting event upon which thousands of pounds were wagered.

The greatest of all the " tea races " took place in 1866. Five clippers left Foochow on the same day. After travelling 14,000 miles, *Ariel* and *Taeping* docked within twenty minutes of each other, ninety-one days later. *Serica* was only an hour and a half behind them.

The race was declared a dead-heat, the three captains sharing the prize of £100 and the bonus of ten shillings for each ton of tea carried.

The clippers sailed, at times, faster than twenty knots.* Their captains were popular heroes and many stories were told of them. It was said that one captain fitted padlocks on his sails when he went to bed at night so that no one could reduce sail and slow down his ship !

More and more steamships came into use during the first half of the nineteenth century, but clippers could outsail the fastest of them, and it was many years before sail was replaced by steam.

* A knot is a speed of one nautical mile (6080 ft.) per hour.

" Ariel " and " Taeping " racing through home waters

Loading a packet ship before she crosses the Atlantic

37. ATLANTIC PACKETS

Regular trips across the North Atlantic had begun at the end of the 1812 war, and in 1816 the Black Ball Line was running services between New York and Liverpool. Ships used on such services were called *packet ships* because they carried packets of mail. Today we call them *liners*.

The Black Ball packets were built for speed, with slender hulls five and a half times as long as they were in the beam. Their average time for the eastward voyage from New York to Liverpool, helped by the westerly winds which blow over the Atlantic, was twenty-one days. Their average time for the return journey was thirty-three days.

The packets were usually three-masters. In calm weather they set five sails on each mast, and staysails and studding sails as well.

The earliest packets were flush-decked, having no forecastle or poop. About 1830 they began to have poop decks with passenger cabins below them.

At this time great numbers of people were moving from Europe to make their home in the United States. Most of these emigrants travelled below decks crowded together like cattle, in filthy conditions.

These passengers had to carry their own food. If a ship made a slow voyage, their rations grew short. One ship, *Diamond*, with 180 emigrants aboard, took one hundred days to sail to New York from Liverpool. Seventeen of her passengers died of starvation.

The emigrants were often ignorant people for whom the captain cared little. The crew told them fearful stories of life at sea. The sailors said that if the weather became rough, the captain would blow a whistle. Then the ship would be cut in half and the front half go on, leaving the back half behind!

When storms blew, the hatches were battened down, and in the darkness the wretched travellers huddled, seasick and frightened, some cursing while others prayed. Sometimes there were outbreaks of disease and a hundred bodies might be cast overboard in a few days.

The best packets had a top speed of about 12 knots. They were driven so hard that they sometimes crossed the ocean in sixteen days. But, in bad weather, forty days was not unusual.

The sailing packets provided the cheapest means of travel until 1850. Then the Inman Line began to carry emigrants cheaply in iron screw steamers.

By 1870 there were few sailing ships left on the Atlantic Ferry. They had lost the fight for trade. The *Red Jacket* sailed from New York to Liverpool in thirteen days one hour in 1853—a remarkable feat. But two years earlier the *Pacific* of the Collins Line had made the same voyage in nine days twenty hours, under steam.

Serving food on a ship carrying emigrants to America

" Thermopylae ", a famous clipper

38. THE LAST DAYS OF SAIL

After the opening of the Suez Canal in 1869, steamers began to take over from clippers on routes to the East. The canal was of no use to sailing ships. They could not easily pass through it, nor would they find favourable winds on the route through the Mediterranean and the Red Sea.

But clippers still sailed to Australia, for on the last stages of that long voyage steamers were unable to obtain coal.

Clippers began to race home with the wool crop from Australia. Two of the most famous to do this were the *Thermopylae* and the *Cutty Sark*, which, in 1872, had a memorable race from China. The *Cutty Sark* lost her rudder on that occasion but still reached home within seven days of her rival.

In 1877 they raced home from Australia. The *Cutty Sark* reached London in seventy-one days, eleven days ahead of the *Thermopylae*. The *Cutty Sark* is preserved today on the Thames at Greenwich.

The last of the clippers, including the *Cutty Sark*, were built with iron frames and wooden planking, but after 1850 some of the clippers carrying wool from Australia had iron hulls. They were bigger than the tea clippers but not so fast.

About 1884, steel-hulled sailing ships appeared. Steel being lighter than iron, steel ships could be built bigger. This was important, for only the biggest sailing ships could compete with the steamships.

Three masts could not carry any more sail, so, to obtain more power, the new steel ships used sails on four masts. The bonaventure mizzen came back as the *jigger* on the four-masted barque, *Great Republic*.

When steamers took over the wool trade, sailing ships still brought grain from Australia by way of Cape Horn and, until the opening of the Panama Canal in 1915, sailing ships carried grain from the west coast of the U.S.A. to the east.

But, from the beginning of the twentieth century, the doom of the sailing ships was sealed. In an attempt to save trade from the steamship, schooners were designed to be run by only a few men so that cargo would be carried more cheaply. For example, the only seven-masted

The " Cutty Sark "

schooner ever built, the *Thomas W. Lawson*, was run by a crew of sixteen. But still trade went to the steamship because it could be relied on to deliver its cargo on time.

" Thomas W. Lawson ", the only seven-masted schooner ever built

PART FOUR : THE AGE OF STEAM

39. THE COMING OF STEAM

In 1736, twenty years after the first successful steam engine had been built, an English clock-maker, Jonathan Hulls, built a boat driven by steam-power. Tested on the River Avon, it was not a success, and Hulls was forced to abandon the project.

Hulls' steamboat

The first successful steamboat was built in 1783 by a French nobleman, the Marquis de Jouffroy. It was driven by paddle-wheels, one on each side of the hull. But the Marquis, like Hulls, ran out of money and had to give up his experiments.

At this time lordly sailing ships carried the world's merchandise and defended the interests of sea-faring powers. Few people suspected that one day they would be replaced by steamships made of iron or steel.

When an enthusiast known as " Iron-mad " Wilkinson launched the first iron vessel in 1787, a crowd turned up for the event jeering : " Iron can't swim ! " They could hardly believe their eyes when they saw that Wilkinson's barge, *Trial*, did not sink.

One man who had faith in steam was John Fitch, an American engineer. In 1787 he launched a steamboat driven by twelve oars, six on each side. Three years later, he built a better vessel driven by three oars at the stern.

Fitch's second boat could travel at 8 m.p.h. With it he began services on the Delaware River between Philadelphia and Trenton. But few people would trust themselves to the " new-fangled fire-boat ". Unable to raise the money to build an even better boat, Fitch killed himself.

Fitch's steamboat of 1790

The " Charlotte Dundas "

40. EARLY PADDLE-STEAMERS

The forerunner of modern steam-ships was the *Charlotte Dundas*, built in 1801 by a Scottish engineer, William Symington. She was driven by a paddle-wheel at the stern.

The *Charlotte Dundas* was intended for use as a tug on the Forth-Clyde Canal, and in March 1802 she towed two seventy-ton barges twenty miles in six hours. This delighted Lord Dundas, for whom she had been built, but the owners of the canal were not so pleased.

They said that waves caused by the steamboat would damage the banks of the canal. So, after that trial run, she was never used again.

The trials of the *Charlotte Dundas* were watched by an American engineer, Robert Fulton. Afterwards he went back to New York and built the *Clermont*, a steamboat driven by two paddle-wheels, one on each side of the hull.

On her maiden voyage the *Clermont*, or "Fulton's Folly", as people called her, steamed away upstream, clanking, splashing and puffing out great clouds of smoke, a shocking sight to the simple fishermen and farmers. Many of them bolted into the woods to hide until she had gone round the next bend, and went home to tell of the "ole ribber debbil" they had seen go by.

In 1807 the *Clermont* began to carry passengers on regular services between New York and Albany, on the Hudson River. She travelled at four and a half miles per hour.

The " Clermont " on her maiden voyage

The " Comet ", 1812

41. BELL'S " COMET "

A Scotsman, Henry Bell, tried to interest the Royal Navy in ocean-going steamships, but their Lordships of the Admiralty declared that novelties of that kind were not likely to be of any use !

Bell was undismayed. In 1812, he launched the first steamship to carry passengers in Britain. This was the *Comet*, a little vessel only forty feet long, driven by two paddle-wheels. She could travel at 9 m.p.h. under steam. Her long thin smoke-stack was designed to carry a sail in case the engine should break down.

With the *Comet*, Bell started regular passenger services on the River Clyde.

By 1815, steamers appeared on the Thames, and, five years later, there was a cross-Channel service.

A newspaper advertisement for the first passenger steamship service in Britain

*Smoke from the " Savannah's "
funnels made sailors think that
the ship was on fire*

42. THE FIRST OCEAN-GOING STEAMSHIPS

In 1819 a ship from the U.S.A. caused a sensation by using steam-power when crossing the North Atlantic. She was the *Savannah*, a three-masted sailing ship fitted with a steam-engine and paddle-wheels. The paddle-wheels could be stowed on deck when not in use.

The *Savannah* crossed from New York to Liverpool in twenty-seven days, during which she used her paddles for only eighty hours. But that was long enough to give passing vessels a shock. The sailors of one ship even thought that the *Savannah* was on fire !

By this time little steamships were being put into use on rivers and canals and in coastal waters. In 1825, the General Steam Navigation Company was commencing its trading across the North Sea.

Even so, few people thought that the steamship was going to take the place of the sailing ship on long voyages. The problem was how to carry sufficient fuel for the engines and leave room for cargo as well.

The first real steamship to cross any ocean was the *Royal William*, a wooden vessel built in Canada. In 1831 she paddled across the Atlantic from Nova Scotia to the Isle of Wight in twenty-five days. In that time she used 324 tons of coal—enough to keep the fire in your home burning for a lifetime !

Six years later, the *William Fawcett*, first of the P. & O. Line, steamed from Falmouth to Gibraltar, and founded the service to India and the Far East.

The " Sirius ", the first ship to cross the Atlantic under continuous steam-power

43. THE " SIRIUS " AND THE " GREAT WESTERN "

Isambard Kingdom Brunel was a man of grand ideas. He was busy building the Great Western Railway from London to Bristol, a distance of 112 miles, but he was looking much farther ahead. The railway was hardly started before he said to the directors : " Why not extend it to America ? Let's build a Great Western steamship to carry the passengers the rest of the way."

It seemed impossible for a ship to carry enough fuel for the voyage of 3300 miles to New York, 1000 miles farther away than Nova Scotia. But Brunel believed that it could be done, for better steam-engines were being built which used less fuel.

The " Great Western "

He began work on the *Great Western*, a big wooden ship, 236 feet long and 35 feet in the beam, with four masts rigged fore and aft. At the same time a ship named *British Queen* was being built at Liverpool to win the honour of the first steam crossing from Britain to New York.

When the company building her found out that the *Great Western* would be ready before their own ship, they hastily obtained a steamer named *Sirius* which had been built to sail between London and Ireland. They filled every inch of space available on board with coal, and, on April 5, 1838, the *Sirius* steamed out of Liverpool bound for New York.

Furniture, planking and spars were burned to keep the engines of the " Sirius " running

The *Sirius*, 208 feet in length, was a two-masted vessel, square-rigged on foremast and fore-and-aft rigged on the mainmast. Strong headwinds met her in the Atlantic, and the crew began to mutiny, but the captain drove them back to work at the point of a pistol.

The *Sirius* completed the crossing of the Atlantic in eighteen days ten hours at an average speed of 6.7 knots, thus becoming the first ship to cross the Atlantic under continuous steam-power.

When she steamed into New York harbour, all her coal had been used; furniture, planking and spars were being burnt to keep the engines running !

Brunel's *Great Western* left Bristol three days after the *Sirius* had set out. She kept up an average speed of 8.8 knots and arrived only a few hours after her rival, with plenty of coal to spare.

44. TRANS-ATLANTIC MAIL STEAMERS: THE CUNARD LINE

The news of what the *Sirius* and the *Great Western* had done caused a sensation. People had to change their ideas about steamships. The British Government was so impressed that it decided that trans-Atlantic mail should now be carried by steamship instead of sailing ship.

The job of carrying it went to Samuel Cunard, a Nova Scotia shipowner. So in 1840 the famous Cunard Steamship Company was started with four ships—*Britannia, Arcadia, Caledonia* and *Columbia*. They were wooden paddle-steamers about 200 feet long, rigged as three-masted barques.

The *Britannia* crossed from Liverpool to Boston in about fourteen days and

Samuel Cunard, 1787–1865

did the return voyage in about ten with the help of the westerly winds that usually blow over the North Atlantic.

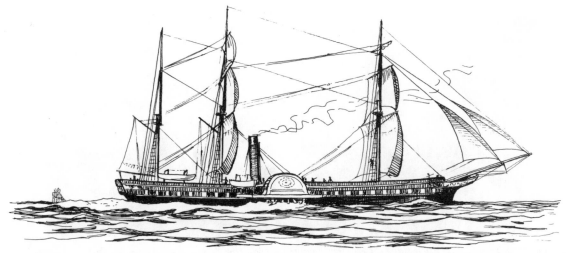

The " Britannia ", the first steamship of the Cunard Steamship Company to cross the Atlantic

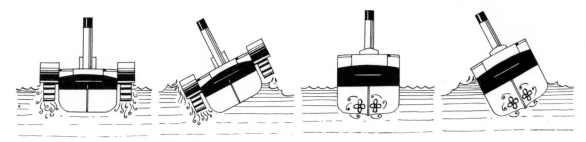

When a paddle-steamer heels over, one paddle is lifted out of the water, and is useless

A screw, or propeller, is more effective because it stays under water

45. EARLY SCREW STEAMERS

Meantime, engineers were trying to find a better way of using steam-power in ships. The clumsy paddle-wheels were often damaged in rough seas, and when a ship rolled from side to side, each wheel in turn was lifted clear of the water.

Several people tried to use some form of under-water propeller or screw, believing this would be an improvement on paddle-wheels. A Middlesex farmer, Francis Pettit Smith, was successful. In 1838 he fitted a screw to a steamer named *Archimedes* which sailed round Britain.

Screw v. Paddle. A tug-of-war between two sloops of the Navy, " Rattler " and " Alecto " in 1845. " Rattler " (screw-driven) dragged " Alecto " astern at the rate of 2 knots for 3 miles

" Great Britain ", *the first iron ship to cross the Atlantic*

The first screw-driven steamer to cross the Atlantic Ocean was an iron ship designed by Brunel, the *Great Britain*. In 1845 she steamed from Liverpool to New York in fourteen days twenty-one hours at an average speed of 9.3 knots.

Three hundred and twenty-two feet in length, the *Great Britain* was the biggest ship afloat in her earliest days. She carried six masts, all of them except the second rigged fore and aft.

The *Great Britain* was the first iron ship to cross the Atlantic, and, by a strange chance, she proved to the scoffers that an iron hull was better and safer than a wooden one.

A paddle-wheel

In 1846 she ran ashore on the coast of Ireland, and there she remained for eleven months at the mercy of the weather. A wooden ship would have been pounded to pieces by the waves, but the *Great Britain* was eventually refloated.

The *Great Britain* later did service on the route to Australia. In 1882, when bigger and better steamships had been built, she was refitted as a full-rigged sailing ship. Four years later she limped to the Falkland Isles after battling through a terrible storm off Cape Horn. She never put to sea again, but her hull was used as a coal hulk until 1937, ninety-four years after her launching.

A four-bladed screw

The " Great Eastern ", launched in 1858, had a crew of 400

46. THE " GREAT IRON SHIP "

Brunel followed the *Great Britain* with the greatest of all the iron ships, the *Great Eastern*. This massive vessel, five times as big as any other ship afloat in her day, took four years to build. She was launched at Millwall in 1858.

From the start, she was unlucky. She was so big—680 feet long and 83 feet in the beam—that she had to be launched sideways. The first attempt to launch her failed, and two men were killed. When she finally put to sea, an explosion off Hastings killed six of her crew.

These and other accidents gave her a bad reputation among seamen, which grew worse later when her captain was killed in an accident on Southampton water. Rumour said that the *Great Eastern* was haunted by a ghost.

She was fitted with a screw as well as paddle-wheels. She had five funnels, and six masts from which could be spread 6500 square yards of canvas. To identify her masts, the sailors called them " Monday, Tuesday, Wednesday, Thursday, Friday and Saturday ". All carried fore-and-aft rig. " Tuesday " and " Wednesday " carried square rig as well.

The launching chains and paddle of the " Great Eastern "

The *Great Eastern* was intended for use on the route to Ceylon. She could carry enough coal to steam 22,000 miles, and also 4000 passengers, a crew of 400, and 6000 tons of cargo. But in fact she was never used on that route. She cost one million pounds to build and the company formed to run the services went bankrupt.

Her early career was a series of accidents and when she crossed to New York in 1860 she carried only thirty-five paying passengers and a cargo of 5000 gross bottles of sauce. She made the voyage in ten and a half days for an average speed of fourteen knots, and returned in the record time of nine days four hours.

In 1861 she steamed from New York to Liverpool with 5000 tons of cargo worth £25,000—the largest cargo a ship had ever carried. But she was not a success on the Atlantic Ferry. She cost so much to run that her owners lost money on her voyages.

Between 1865 and 1873 the *Great Eastern* was employed in laying telegraph cables across the Atlantic, but still her owners were unable to make her pay her way. In 1886 she was hired out as a floating fairground at Liverpool, and half a million people visited her. A year later she was sold for scrap iron.

Isambard Kingdom Brunel, builder of the "Great Eastern"

The *Great Eastern* had two bottoms —a fact which saved her from sinking when, in 1862, she struck a rock near New York. When she was being broken up, between these two bottoms were found the skeletons of two workmen who had vanished while she was being built.

Sea-faring men nodded their heads sagely when they heard of this. "She was an unlucky ship," they said, "and no wonder".

The grand saloon of the "Great Eastern" during a storm

The " Bothnia " carried sails in case her engines broke down

47. THE SHAPE OF MODERN SHIPS

The earliest steamships carried sails for use when winds were favourable, and for a long time the steamship looked like a sailing ship fitted with paddle-wheels and funnels.

Straight

Raked

Maierform

Shapes of bows

But the *Bothnia*, of 1874, an iron ship driven by a screw, carried sails only in case her engine broke down. Her hull was unlike a sailing ship's, the bow rising almost straight up from the water. By the time of the *Bothnia*

the pattern of the modern steamship had been set. The same shape can still be seen in some of the mighty liners of today.

Builders of sailing ships, master craftsmen though many of them were, often worked without any proper plans. Today the building of ships is an exact science. For instance, before the shape of the *Queen Mary*'s hull was finally decided, 8000 tests were made with models.

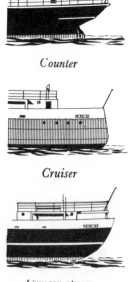

Counter

Cruiser

Cruiser spoon

Shapes of sterns

48. THE ENGINES OF MODERN SHIPS

In 1885 Charles Parsons started work on a new type of steam-engine. Instead of using steam to push a lever which turned a wheel, he produced an engine in which the steam itself turned a wheel. This engine, which did not waste so much power, was called the *steam turbine*.

Parsons offered his invention to the Navy, but the Lords of the Admiralty showed little interest in it. Later, during the Naval Review of 1897, a small ship suddenly appeared among the battleships of the fleet and began to race up and down the lines. Fast destroyers set off after this intruder but it left them all far behind.

It was the *Turbinia,* a steam yacht fitted with Parsons' invention, and it travelled at almost 35 knots. The

The " Victorian ", launched in 1904

inventor had taken this startling step to show the Lords of the Admiralty how well the steam turbine worked.

It worked so well at high speeds that it was soon used not only by the Royal Navy but also by all fast steamships. The first Atlantic liner to be driven by turbines was the *Victorian*, launched by the Allen Line in 1904.

" Turbinia " racing down the lines at the Naval Review of 1897

The French liner " Normandie " which was driven by turbo-electric power

The famous French liner, the *Normandie*, launched in 1932, was driven by turbo-electric power, a system by which the turbines turn dynamos to produce electricity and the electricity is used to drive the propellers.

The big ships of today are still driven by steam-engines, but most of them burn oil instead of coal. Although oil is more expensive, it is more easily taken aboard than coal and cleaner to use. Coaling was a most unpleasant task and it took several days afterwards to clean the ship.

As long ago as 1910 the first ship was launched with an engine like a motor car's but using diesel oil instead of petrol. Since then a number of big liners have been built to use diesel engines. One reached a speed of $23\frac{1}{2}$ knots, but the diesel engine could not match the speed and power of the modern steam engine.

The first successful turbo-electric ship was the U.S.S. *Jupiter* of 1913. Today turbo-electric power is used by a number of large ships. The *Canberra*, shown on page 78, has turbo-electric engines.

Ships of the future will be driven by nuclear power, but the use of atomic reactors involves many problems, notably those arising from the danger of radiation.

The first nuclear-powered merchant ship, the *Savannah*, was launched in the U.S.A. in 1959. The *Savannah*, fuelled with uranium oxide, can operate for three and a half years, covering 350,000 miles, before refuelling. Her speed is $20\frac{1}{4}$ knots.

" Savannah ", the world's first nuclear-powered merchant ship

49. THE BLUE RIBAND

The story of the further development of the steamship can be summed up in the story of the Atlantic Ferry—the most important sea route in the world.

In 1881, for the first time, a ship built of steel crossed the ocean—the Cunard liner, *Servia*.

In 1888, the *Philadelphia* was driven by two screws instead of one. She became the first ship to cross the ocean in less than six days.

In 1904, the first steam turbine ship appeared on the Atlantic Ferry, the *Virginian*. She was driven by three screws. Four screws were first used by the *Aquitania*, which was built in 1913. The same number are used by today's biggest liner, the *Queen Elizabeth*.

The Blue Riband of the Atlantic is held by the ship that has made the fastest passage across the ocean between Europe and the U.S.A. Since 1934, a trophy has been awarded.

The first holder was the *Britannia*. In 1840, she made the westerly crossing in 14 days 8 hours for an average speed of 8.5 knots and returned in ten days for an average of 10.5 knots.

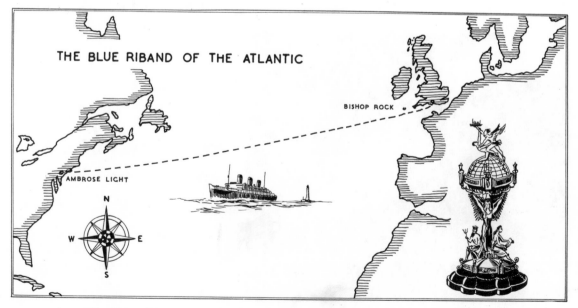

The Blue Riband Trophy is awarded for the fastest Atlantic crossing

" Queen Mary " steams into New York harbour

Today the Blue Riband is held by the U.S. liner *United States,* which, in 1952, crossed from New York to the Scilly Isles in 3 days 10 hours 40 minutes for an average speed of 35.5 knots.

Here is a list of ships which have held the Blue Riband since 1910 :

The " United States "

Date	Ship	Country
1910–28	*Mauretania*	Great Britain
1929	*Bremen*	Germany
1930	*Europa*	Germany
1933	*Bremen*	Germany
1933	*Rex*	Italy
1935	*Normandie*	France
1936	*Queen Mary*	Great Britain
1937	*Normandie*	France
1938	*Queen Mary*	Great Britain
1952	*United States*	U.S.A.

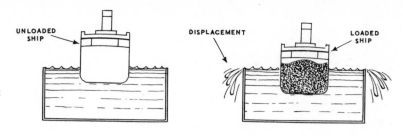

Displacement tonnage is a measure of the weight of a ship. It is the weight of the water displaced when a ship is fully loaded

UNLOADED SHIP

DISPLACEMENT

LOADED SHIP

50. SHIP'S TONNAGE

The size of a ship is often expressed in terms of *tonnage*. This may be misleading, for there are many different kinds of tonnage.

Until the seventeenth century the size of ships bringing wine from Bordeaux was expressed in the number of tuns of wine they could carry, a tun cask containing 252 gallons and occupying 60 cubic feet of space. So " tuns burthen ", as it was called, was a rough measure of the cargo space in a ship.

Today the space in a ship is still expressed in tons, one ton being 100 cubic feet. *Gross tonnage* is a measure of all the space in a ship, with certain exceptions. *Net tonnage* is a measure of all the space in a ship used for carrying passengers or cargo. But *displacement tonnage* is a measure of weight. It is the weight of the water displaced when a ship is fully loaded. The amount of water displaced by a ship when not loaded gives her displacement in light condition. The difference between these two figures is, of course, the weight of the cargo. It is called *deadweight tonnage*.

The diagram shows the growth of steamships in terms of gross tonnage. The sailing ships have been included for comparison. The gross tonnage figures are approximate.

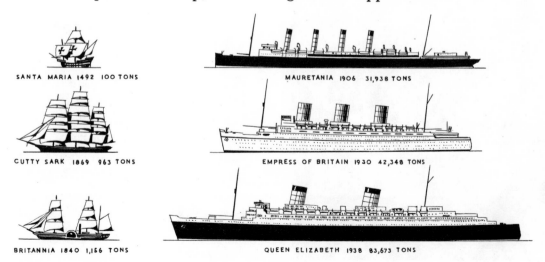

SANTA MARIA 1492 100 TONS

CUTTY SARK 1869 963 TONS

BRITANNIA 1840 1,156 TONS

MAURETANIA 1906 31,938 TONS

EMPRESS OF BRITAIN 1930 42,348 TONS

QUEEN ELIZABETH 1938 83,673 TONS

" Queen Elizabeth 2 "

65,863 tons, 963 ft. long
twin screws
two 55,000 h.p. turbines
cruising speed 28·5 knots

51. TRAVEL BY SEA TODAY

Nowadays, people in a hurry travel by air, so the role of the passenger ship has changed. Cunard's *QE2*, which made her maiden voyage in May 1969, is designed for both the North Atlantic crossing and for " sun cruises " in winter. Hence, her dimensions and draught enable her to use the Panama and Suez canals and most ports in cruising areas. She is really a superb hotel, with luxurious rooms (not cabins) for some 2000 passengers. There are lounges, restaurants, playrooms, discotheques, four swimming-pools, twenty-two lifts, a theatre, library, hospital, kennels, shops and even a printing-press for the daily news-paper.

Sea travel is not only more comfort-able than ever before, it is safer. *QE2* has a safety-control room with instruments that give warning of any unusual condition, even of minute changes in atmosphere and temperature in any part of the ship. All the radar, navigation and echo-sounding equipment is duplicated, so that if one instrument fails, another takes over.

A new type of ship is the hovercraft, invented by an Englishman, C. Cockerell. It skims over water, land and ice on a cushion of air fired downwards by air-jets and travels at 50 to 100 m.p.h. So far, it is used mainly to ferry passengers and cars across the English Channel.

A hovercraft

MUSEUMS IN BRITAIN WHICH CONTAIN MODELS OF SHIPS

ANNAN (Scotland)   Annan Museum
DARTMOUTH (Devon)   Borough Museum
EDINBURGH   Royal Scottish Museum
GLASGOW   Art Gallery and Museum, Kelvingrove
GREAT YARMOUTH (Norfolk)   The Sailors' Home Museum
HASTINGS (Sussex)   Old Town Hall Museum
HULL (Yorkshire)   Fisheries and Shipping Museum
LONDON   National Maritime Museum, Greenwich
NEWCASTLE (Northumberland)   Museum of Science and Engineering
PLYMOUTH (Devon)   City Museum
PORTSMOUTH (Hampshire)   The Victory Museum
ROCHESTER (Kent)   Public Museum
SHOREHAM (Sussex)   Marlipins Museum
SOUTH SHIELDS (County Durham)   Public Library and Museum
WHITBY (Yorkshire)   Literary and Philosophical Museum

SOME MORE BOOKS ABOUT SHIPS

DISCOVERING SAILING SHIPS C. G. France U.L.P. 1955
SHIPS R. Hope Batsford 1958
THE STORY OF SHIPS S. E. Ellacott Methuen 1958
SHIPS J. S. Murphy Oxford 1959
LOOK AT SHIPS S. Ramsey Hamilton 1960
SHIPS A. B. Cornwell Ward Lock 1961
FROM CORACLES TO CUNARDERS L. E. Snellgrove Longmans 1962
BRITISH TRAMPS, COASTERS AND COLLIERS L. Dunn Odhams 1962
THE STUDY BOOK OF SHIPS E. Baxter Bodley Head 1963
BRITISH SAILING WARSHIPS J. J. Colledge Ian Allan 1964
SHIPS E. W. Brown Wheaton 1965
THE SAILING SHIP J. de Hartog Hamlyn 1965
SHIPS F. G. Kay Baker 1966
THE STORY OF SHIPS G. Fouillé Hamlyn 1968
SHIPS Frank Knight Benn 1969

INDEX